PETER ILJITCH TSCHAIKOWSKY

"1812"
OVERTURE SOLENNEl ... EMNE
OP. 49

The work was composed in 1880 ... All-Russian Exhibition of Arts and ... in Moscow, but first performed on th... August, 1882, at the consecration of the Cathedral of the Saviour in Moscow, which was built in commemoration of the Russian victory over Napoleon in 1812. The first performance is said to have been given in the open air by an orchestra of several hundred players, the timpani part being executed by a battery of artillery.

The overture is "programme music", giving a musical illustration of the events of that crucial year in Russian and European history.

... n ocasión de ... artes y oficios, ... se ejecutó por primera vez el 8 de agosto del 1882 en la ceremonia de consagración de la catedral del Salvador en Moscou, construída en conmemoración de la victoria rusa sobre Napoleón en 1812. Cuéntase que la primera ejecución tuvo lugar al aire libre, con una orquesta de varios centenares de ejecutantes y la parte de los "timpani" confiada a una "batería de artillería".

Es un ejemplo de música descriptiva o "de programa" que evoca los acontecimientos de aquel año crucial en la historia de Rusia y de Europa.

ANALYSIS

INTRODUCTION. A Russian ecclesiastical anthem opens

ANÁLISIS

INTRODUCCIÓN. Un himno eclesiástico ruso sirve de introducción.

Ex.1   Vla.Vc.   *mf*

A plaintive motive is the foreboding of the coming plight (p. 3, bar 36).

Un motivo plañidero parece anunciar las duras pruebas por venir (p. 3, comp. 36).

Ex.2   Ob.Solo   *f*

It leads to a climax reached in the solemn passage of the bassoon, violoncello and bass (p. 12).

FIRST PART (p. 13, bar 80). Martial music sounds in the distance. The storm of war rages in Europe. A vehement motive illustrates its fury (p. 16, bar 97)

Alcanza su climax en el solemne pasaje de fagote, violoncelo y contrabajo (p. 12).

PRIMERA PARTE (p. 13, comp. 80). A distancia se oye música de carácter marcial. El azote de la guerra está devastando Europa. Un motivo vehemente ilustra su fúria (p. 16, comp. 97)

Ex.3   Vl.I

and from the turmoil gradually rises the Marseillaise (p. 21, bar 120, horns) until it dominates in triumphant "fff" (p. 34, bar 150).

SECOND PART. Suddenly the scene changes. Holy Russia is far away from the events, a peaceful country with the peasants singing (p. 37, bar 165)

emergiendo gradualmente de la agitación la melodía de la "Marsellesa" (p. 21, comp. 120, trompas) hasta dominar por fin triunfalmente en "fff" (p. 34, comp. 150).

SEGUNDA PARTE. Cambia la escena de pronto. La santa Rusia, a inmensa distancia de los sangrientos acontecimientos, vive en profunda paz ; sus campesinos cantando (p. 37, comp. 165)

Ex. 4

and dancing (p. 44, bar 207).

y bailando (p. 44, comp. 207).

Ex. 5

THIRD PART (p. 46, bar 224). But there is war. Motive Ex. 3, a trumpet call and a rolling side drum efface the picture of idyllic country life and the Marseillaise sounds again (p. 47). Napoleon's Great Army is on the march and stands at the gate. Still they sing and dance in Russia (p. 61) but the French armies have invaded the country and their war call mingles with the dance (p. 66). The Russians leave the plough and take up arms, the fury of the battle is unleashed (p. 71) with the Marseillaise still dominating but overcome in the furious onslaught of the Russian armies.

TERCERA PARTE (p. 46, comp. 224). Pero ahí está la guerra. El motivo ej. 3, un toque de trompeta y un redoble de tambor borran de pronto la printura de la apacible vida campesina y de nuevo resuena la "Marsellesa" (p. 47). El Gran Ejército de Napoleón está en marcha. Todavía se canta y se baila en Rusia (p. 61) pero las tropas francesas han invadido ya el país y los toques bélicos se mezclan ya con los aires de danza (p. 66). Los campesinos rusos abandonan el arado por las armas y se desata la fúria de la batalla (p. 71) dominando todavía la "Marsellesa" pero por fin sojuzgada ante la furiosa avalancha de los ejércitos rusos.

FOURTH PART (p. 76, bar 358). Victory is won. The thoughts turn to the Saviour (theme Ex. 1 in the whole band) and to the fatherland (Russian National Anthem p. 83, bar 388, bassoons, horns, trombones and low strings).

CUARTA PARTE (p. 76, comp. 358). La victoria ha sido alcanzada. Vuelve otra vez el pensamiento hacia el Salvador (tema ej. 1 en madera y metal) y hacia la patria (himno nacional ruso, p. 83, comp. 388, fagotes, trompas, trombones y cuerda grave).

TRANSPOSING INSTRUMENTS

INSTRUMENTOS TRANSPOSITORES

Transposing instruments are those which are used in various pitches. The actual sound, therefore, differs from the notation. The following examples are given in order to facilitate the reading of the score. The big notes indicate the notation used, the small notes the actual sounds produced

Instrumentos transpositores son los que se usan en afinaciones varias ; por consiguiente su sonido real difiere de la nota escrita. Los ejemplos siguientes se dan para facilitar la lectura de la partitura—las notas mayores corresponden a la notación escrita, las notas pequeñas corresponden al sonido real

FLAUTO PICCOLO (Flautín)

CORNO INGLESE (Cor anglais)
Wagner, The Flying Dutchman, (El buque fantasma).

CLARINET IN Bb (Clarinete en Sib)
Beethoven, Symph. No. 3

CLARINET IN A (Clarinete en La)
Mendelssohn, Midsummer Night's Dream (Sueño de una noche de verano)

DOUBLE BASSOON (Contrafagot)
(and Double Bass) (y contrabajo)

HORN (Trompa)
in Bb (Sib)(alto) Bb (Sib) basso A(La)
See Clarinets. Véanse los clarinetes

HORN (Trompa) in G (Sol) and F (Fa)
Mozart, Symph. G minor (Sol menor).

Tschaikowsky, Symph. No. 4.

HORN (Trompa)in E (Mi) Eb (Mib), D(Re)
Beethoven, Symph. No. 7

Beethoven, Symph. No 3.

Schubert, Symph. B minor (Si menor).

HORN (Trompa)
in C (Do) alto) C(Do) basso)   C (Do) basso

TRUMPET (Trompeta)
in Bb(Sib) A(La) F (Fa) E (mi) Eb (Mib)

For examples see Clarinets and horns (one octave higher) Para ejemplos véanse clarinetes y trompas (una octava más alto)

CLEFS — CLAVES

SOPRANO. Clave de Sol

ALTO   Clave de Contralto
See the viola parts
Véanse las partes de viola

TENOR. Clave de Tenor
to be found in bassoon, trombone and violoncello parts hállase en las partes de fagote, trombón y violoncelo.

TSCHAIKOWSKY

"1812"

OUVERTURE SOLENNELLE

OP. 49

Distributed By
HAL•LEONARD®
CORPORATION
7777 W. BLUEMOUND RD. P.O. BOX 13819 MILWAUKEE, WI 53213

"1812"
Ouverture Solennelle

P. Tschaikowsky, Op. 49
1840-1893

8

12

14

90

20

22

B. & H. 8735

24

26

B. & H. 8735

32

B. & H. 8735

B. & H. 8735

38

42

B. & H. 8735

47

210

B. & H. 8735

220

51

B. & H. 8735

54

B. & H. 8735

55

B. & H. 8735

59

B. & H. 8735

62

64

B. & H. 8735

70

B. & H. 8735

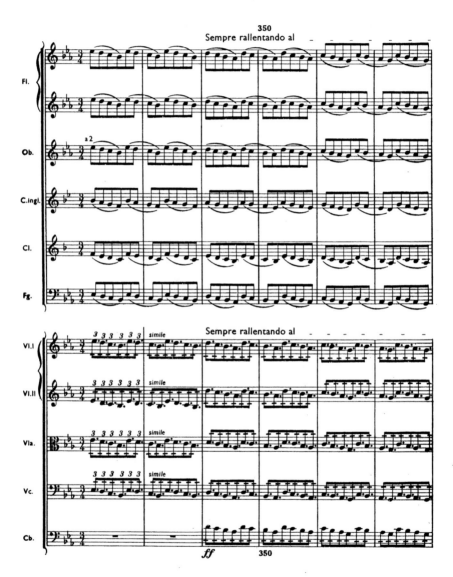

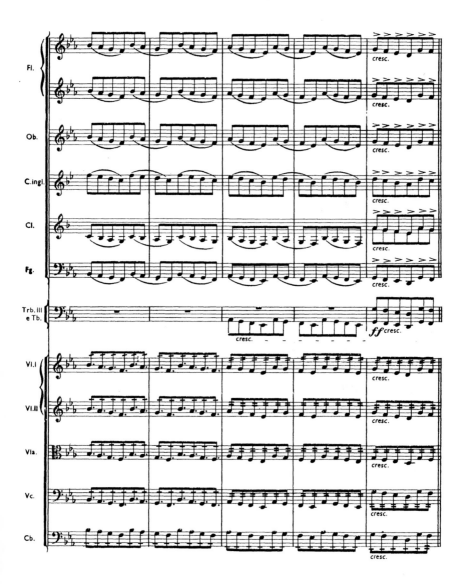

80

360

B. & H. 8735

81

B. & H. 8735

84
Bd.
Picc.
Fl.
a 2
Ob.
C.ingl.
Cl.
Fg.
Cor.
Pist.
Tr.
Trb. e Tb.
Timp.
Pttl.
G.C.
Camp.
Vl.I
Vl.II
Vla.
Vc.
Cb.

B. & H. 8735